CIRCLES OF MADNESS

CIRCLES OF MADNESS
CÍRCULOS DE LOCURA

MOTHERS OF THE PLAZA DE MAYO
MADRES DE LA PLAZA DE MAYO

PHOTOGRAPHS BY
ALICIA D'AMICO AND ALICIA SANGUINETTI

POEMS BY MARJORIE AGOSÍN

TRANSLATED BY CELESTE KOSTOPULOS-COOPERMAN

WHITE PINE PRESS

PQ
7763
,E5
A75
1992

Printed in the United States of America.

ISBN 1-877727-17-2

Book design by Watershed Design.

White Pine books are printed on acid-free paper.

Gifts 8/97

Publication of this book was made possible, in part, by grants from the National
Endowment for the Arts, the New York State Council on the Arts,
and Wellesley College.

White Pine Press
76 Center Street
Fredonia, New York 14063

CIRCLES OF MADNESS

PREFACE

The "disappeared" of Argentina were in reality men and women, for the most part young people, who were detained by agents of the state during the military dictatorship of 1976-1983 and about whom nothing is known to the present day. The armed forces exercised defacto political power and opted to secretly carry out a sweeping genocide. Those thousands of disappeared detainees were gathered in clandestine detention centers where they were kept in total isolation, savagely tortured, and assassinated in absolute solitude. Their bodies were either incinerated, hurled into the sea, or buried in other equally secret places by the constituents of the army, the navy, and the air force, who tried to commit the perfect crime, i.e., to leave no traces. Their objective was not fulfilled, however, and today, although we cannot know the individual fates of those human beings while the military archives remain closed, we are completely familiar with the system and its authors. Unfortunately, the constitutional government that followed the dictatorship has punished only minimally those responsible for that hypocritical and atrocious crime.

*   *   *

Marjorie Agosín, a poet and writer of refined sensibility, educated both in the United States and in her native country, Chile, and professor of Latin American literature at Wellesley College in Massachusets, evokes in this book the plight of the disappeared Argentines and of their mothers. Her imagination and senses take flight before the photographs of the Mothers of the Plaza de Mayo, who in their rounds carry the pictures of their children. The faces of the mothers and of the children constitute the recurrent theme of these limpid prose poems.

The metaphors follow one another, without stopping, one behind the other, throughout these pages, like variations on a unique central theme: *Then all the mothers approached. . . then I take out my photograph. . . Have you seen my son? she asked me. . . Look, these are the photographs of my children. . . Here are our albums—these are the photographs—of their faces— come closer, do not be afraid. Isn't it true they're very young? She is my daughter.* And what follows are the expressions of love of the mothers who talk with their children, who think about their youthful bodies, their beauty, their words and their songs; about their kisses, their jobs, their hopes and illusions. All of them were known for their selflessness, their boundless generosity and unlimited love, and they were sacrificed by presumptuous uniformed jackals, heralds of death, who were disturbed by their liberty, their happiness, and their defense of life against adversity and injustice.

The pictures of the children and the white kerchiefs of the mothers *that they tie, that are untied, madly whistle, kiss and moan* are the images that inspire the poet and suggest to her unpredictable comparisons which, like all authentic poetry, issue from the soul: *I want a kerchief against injustice so I can cover you, dance with you on the winged banners of peace, fill you up with caresses and make you dream about a memory of your body very close to mine, as if we were two joining fountainheads. She marches, she stretches, and her grief expands, increasingly transforming her into an immense pyramid of sunflowers and dung. She says that she is looking for either her living or her dead. . .There is no mourning for the seeker.* The emphasis is mine, because the absence of a body to mourn is the indescribable agony of this never ending drama—only captured by poetry— for those of us who have a disappeared son or daughter. For this reason, I have read with concentrated emotion these poems of Marjorie Agosín— poems that are not only of grief and death but also of life and hope. They will forever resurrect the memory of the "disappeared" among the living, just as the disappeared will rise from the dead in the House of the Father. It is only fitting, therefore, that they conclude with a memorial and with a *Poem to be Recited in Dreams of the Sea,* in that sea where rest the remains of the thousands of nameless detainees who were thrown from the airplanes of the genocidal agents the people had entrusted with their defense. Marjorie Agosín speaks the truth when she reassures us in the last line of her book that *My words will be transformed into thousands of faces.*

—Emilio F. Mignone
Buenos Aires
July 1990

CIRCLES OF MADNESS

THE DANCERS

The photographs stopped being a means of generating hallucination or mere signs that record the seasons of feeble times. They existed as witnesses to the immediacy of history. Each photograph commemorates the presence of an absence, just as does the search that scrutinizes, interrogates, intrigues, and terrifies. Is there anything more somber than some mothers walking together with a poster filled with the photographs of their dead relatives? These photographs, however, do not give shape to celebrations, to birthdays, to anniversaries, or even to the days of their deaths. These photographs are like extensions of the missing; each snapshot represents an absent body, a body that doesn't judge or even identify the guilty. It is merely a body, prostrated and tied to the body of a mother who lives and carries it publically through the plazas, through the land, just as she carried it in her womb protecting futures.

The photographs of the Mothers of the Plaza de Mayo both represent and present, like an inquiring debate between the bearers of the beloved face that often becomes a portrait that possesses and those who hide the image, devour the presence, make it vanish, and convert it into a melody of calcinatory smoke. It is the perserverance of the women who carry these portraits that creates from the body a piece of life. Thus the vigils visualized in the photo-text, a bearer of a definite presence, are transformed into a silent call. Like the accusatory and famous "Where are they?," they are a question that demands a communal response and that urges an answer not only from the passers-by but also from the sky and from the earth. They are an affirmation of the torturers who roam about freely looking at those faces they, at one time, had made theirs to divest of human life with the perverse goal of making them suffer.

The photographs of Alicia D'Amico and Alicia Sanguinetti postulate an ethic, a way of being, and a presence that does not cry out for only information; the presence of the photographed is already a definite and unadulterated proof of their existence.

There they are, looking at us and seen; there are the eyes, the mouths where words were expressed and loves spoken of. They are there, and we know that they are, but "Where are they?" So when we see them pass by, we ask ourselves, "What are they dreaming or not dreaming about?" The Mothers of the Plaza de Mayo, "What do they talk about among themselves, or do they share prayers of grief because their souls are burdened by the wounds and the memories of their losses?'' But other times, when the sun devours like an irascible accomplice, and we see them together with their heads covered by kerchiefs, they resemble hallucinatory doves that shine in the middle of a nebula and appear singing prayers of life. Because what could be more courageous than carrying a child on the breast so everyone knows it is alive there and that perhaps it eats in the evenings and someone compassionate dares to cover it and to sing to it something that is more than a lullaby?

How can we talk about these phototographs? What language can be used to tell what they tell without exaggeration, without sensationalism, but with a vision that comes directly and from the heart? The Mothers in one of the photographs form a fan of light; they are in the Plaza de Mayo in all the corrupt splendor of its rulers. In yet another photo, we see one of them, alone, very lonely, sitting at a marble table, waiting for her missing with a glass of water, with a flower, and with a lot of light, a queen lost within her kingdom . . .

These prose poems are fragments, homages, threads and images that accompany the powerful art of Alicia D'Amico and Alicia Sanguinetti, as they also accompany the mothers in their strolls through life, putting aside dark vengeance and fears and the question outlined in the eyes of the observers: "Have you seen them or have you not seen them?'' Help these women find their loved one in the poems so that you can tell them that no death is in vain.

The photographs of Alicia D'Amico and Alicia Sanguinetti act both as instruments and as an approach to knowledge that makes us remember that personae go beyond masks.

The photographers transcend the faces of the Mothers of the Plaza de Mayo, as well as those of their children. They do it tastefully and with an exquisite sensitivity and an aesthetic that is an act of love and an unblinking look at the phantasmagoric. They capture both beauty and monstrosity and register them without sentimentality or shock but with a wisdom that is immense and diaphanous.

—Marjorie Agosín

CIRCLES OF MADNESS

Entonces le pidió
que le guardara sus ojos
en el delantal de percal,
y el otro
le pidió que le guardara
sus manos
en su cintura de hilos,
y la otra le pidió
que enterrara sus piernas
en el jardín de las amapolas
entonces se acercaron todas las madres
entonces se abrieron todos los delantales
como un enorme ataúd
con los sonidos del cielo
entonces sólo quedaron los retratos
de los ojos mancos.

Then he asked her
to keep his eyes
in her apron of percale
and the other
asked her to keep
his hands
on her linen waist
and yet another asked her
to bury her legs
in the garden of the butterflies
then all the mothers approached
then all the aprons opened
like an enormous coffin
with sounds coming from the sky
then all that remained were the pictures
of the maimed eyes.

Cuando encendida la luz de la noche,
y el tiempo es una manta de agua viva,
y el cielo otro silencio aún más silencioso,
cuando las paredes retratan las trizaduras de la mala hora
y todos se duermen en las criptas del insomnio
entonces saco mi fotografía
hago el amor con ella,
la desvisto,
la bailo,
la oigo,
acariciándola,
amándola muy así como en un aire muy dulce,
entonces,
le hablo,
le digo: que bueno que has regresado de los infiernos,
hace tanto tiempo
que no nos vemos;
tanto tiempo sin verte
y la coloco junto
a mi pecho,
me pongo a bailar
con mi muerto
y me pongo a soñar con
mi foto.

When the evening light burns
and time is a blanket of living water,
and the sky another silence even more silent,
when the walls depict the shredded fragments of the evil hour
and everyone falls asleep in the crypts of insomnia
then I take out my photograph
I make love to it,
I undress it,
I dance with it,
I hear it,
caressing it,
and loving it much like a spring of fresh water,
then
I talk to it,
and say: how wonderful that you have returned from hell,
it has been a long time
since we have seen each other;
so much time without seeing you
and I place it close
to my chest,
and I begin to dance
with my dead one
and I begin to dream with
my photo.

¿Ha visto a mi hijo? me
preguntó
tenía una cicatriz alumbradora
en las sienes
tenía los labios de rosa
¿Lo ha visto?
me preguntó
¿O tal vez ha visto
mientras alguien enloquecido
hacía estallar su piel en dolores?
¿Ha visto a mi hijo? me
preguntó
aunque sea por un instante,
¿ha visto a mi hijo?
me dijo
(Ha visto a mi
hijo?
me volvió a preguntar.

Have you seen my son?
she asked me.
He had a shining scar
on his temple
and rose-colored lips
Have you seen him?
she asked me.
Or did you perhaps witness
some demented person
making his skin explode in piercing pain?
Have you see my son?
she asked me.
Even if only for an instant,
have you seen my son?
she said.
Have you seen
my son?
she continued to ask.

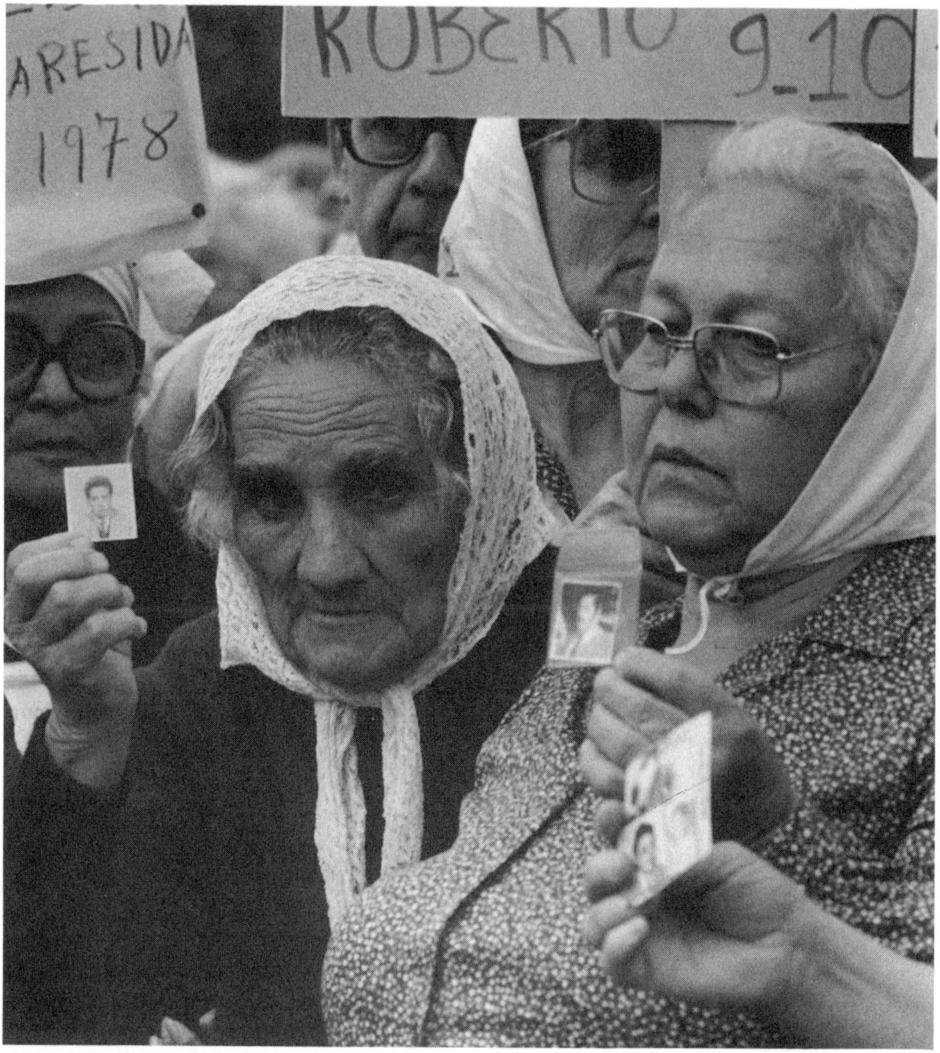
ARESIDA
1978
ROBERTO 9-10

Y a veces me acerco en las puntillas del insomnio mismo,
me detengo
para tocar sus labios
y decirle cosas en secreto
nada demasiado secreto
tan sólo lo que no se le podía decir
mientras lo venían a buscar
mientras lo desnudaban para golpearlo
y dejarlo como una herida en las habitaciones
nebulosas
entonces
yo me acerco
a la orilla misma
de sus labios
que parecen
dos entradas de mar
dos ausencias
que se pueblan de mis palabras
que se estrellan
contra una fotografía
incrustada
en mi alma
como un talismán de mis dolencias.

And sometimes I approach the borders of insomnia
on tiptoe,
I stop
to touch his lips
and to tell him things in secret
nothing too secret
only things that could not be said to him
when they came looking for him
while they undressed him to beat him
and abandon him
like a wounded animal
in the nebulous rooms
then
I approach
the very shore
of his lips
that seem like
two estuaries
two absences
that are filled with my words
that crash
against a photograph
encrusted
in my soul
like a talisman of my sorrows

Mira,
éstas son las fotografías
de mis hijos
aquí tiene un brazo
no sé si será de mi hijo
pero pienso que tal vez sí
que éste es su brazito de almíbar.
Mira aquí están sus piernas,
cortadas, sajadas
rasgadas
pero son sus piernas
o tal vez las piernas de otro.
No temas
son sólo las fotos
dicen que es una forma de identificación
y que a lo mejor si te las
muestran
tú misma me ayudarás a encontrarlo.
Mira estas fotografías
regístralas en los álbumes de la vida.

Look,
these are the photographs
of my children,
this one here has an arm
I don't know if it's my son's,
but I think it might be
that this is his sweet little arm.
Look, here are his legs,
severed, cut
and torn
but they are his legs
or perhaps the legs of another.
Don't be afraid.
They are only photographs.
They say it is a form of identification
and if at best they show them
to you
you will be able to help me find him.
Look at these photographs
and record them in the albums of life.

Aquí están nuestros álbumes
éstas son las fotografías
de los rostros
acérquese, no tenga
miedo
¿es verdad que son muy jóvenes? es mi hija,
mire ésta
Andrea y ésta
es mi hija Paola
somos las madres de los
desaparecidos.
Coleccionamos
sus rostros
en estas fotografías
muchas veces hablamos con ellos,
y nos preguntamos
¿quién acariciará
el pelo de la Graciela?
¿qué habrán hecho con el cuerpecito
de Andrés?
Fíjese que tenián nombres,
les gustaba leer
eran muy jóvenes
ninguno de ellos alcanzó a celebrar
sus dieciocho años,
aquí están sus fotografías,
estos inmensos álbumes
acérquese,
ayúdeme
a lo mejor usted
lo ha visto
y cuando se vaya al extranjero
lleve una de estas fotografías.

Here are our albums,
these are the photographs
of their faces.
Come closer, do not be
afraid.
Isn't it true they're very young?
She is my daughter.
Look at this one.
She is Andrea and this
is my daughter Paola.
We are the mothers of the
disappeared.
We collect
their faces
in these photographs
and we often talk with them
and ask ourselves
Who will caress
Graciela's hair?
What have they done with Andres'
little body?
Notice that they had names,
they liked to read,
they were very young.
None of them ever got to celebrate
their eighteenth birthday.
Here are their photographs,
these immense albums.
Come close,
help me.
Maybe you
have seen him,
and when you travel
take one of these photographs with you.

Cuando me enseñó su fotografía
me dijo
ésta es mi hija
aún no llega a casa
hace diez años que no llega
pero ésta es su fotografía
¿Es muy linda no es cierto?
es una estudiante de filosofía
y aquí está cuando teniá
catorce años
e hizo su primera
comunión
almidonada, sagrada.
ésta es mi hija
es tan bella
todos los días converso con ella
ya nunca llega tarde a casa, yo por eso la reprocho
mucho menos
pero la quiero tantísimo
ésta es mi hija
todas las noches me despido de ella
la beso
y me cuesta no llorar
aunque sé que no llegará
tarde a casa
porque tú sabes, hace años que
no regresa a casa
yo quiero mucho a esta foto
la miro todos los días
me parece ayer cuando
era un angelito de plumas en mis manos
y aquí está toda hecha una dama
una estudiante de filosofía
una desaparecida
pero ¿no es cierto que es tan linda,
que tiene un rostro de angel.
que parece que estuviera viva?

When she showed me her photograph
she said,
This is my daughter.
She still hasn't come home.
She hasn't come home in ten years.
But this is her photograph.
Isn't it true that she is very pretty?
She is a philosophy student
and here she is when she was
fourteen years old
and had her first
communion,
starched, sacred.
This is my daughter.
She is so pretty.
I talk to her every day.
She no longer comes home late, and this is why I reproach her
much less.
But I love her so much.
This is my daughter.
Every night I say goodbye to her.
I kiss her
and it's hard for me not to cry
even though I know she will not come
home late
because as you know, she has not come
home for years.
I love this photo very much.
I look at it every day.
It seems that only yesterday
she was a little feathered angel in my arms
and here she looks like a young lady,
a philosophy student,
another disappeared.
But isn't it true that she is so pretty,
that she has an angel's face,
that it seems as if she were alive?

I

Como un ave migratoria, ella se deplaza entre los muebles
vendados, como si toda la habitación fuera un solo precipicio que
la golpea, que la desdibuja y entre las tinieblas de los
videntes, ella se pregunta sobre la felicidad de aquella sagrada,
casi imaginaria familia.

II

Ilumina los adioses de la pequeña Lila,
recuerda el beso de Claudito,
recuerda los pies, el agua, el ruido de los tiernos ríos, en sus palmas,
las piedras en los rincones de cada bolsillo amado
entonces enciende las lámparas del amor
y pareciera que se desnudara en un lienzo de cantares
y pareciera que ellos lloraran.

III

De sus bocas salen
pájaros,
el nombre de los hijos
y de los hijos
de las otras
y las otras
también dicen el nombre de las otras y otros hijos de otras,
se buscan
se humedecen
abandonadas se recogen,
son las Madres de la Plaza de Mayo.

I

Like a migratory bird, she unfurls herself among the draped
furniture, as if the entire room were a dangerous edge that
erases her, that draws her faded outline, and in the
blindness of those who see, she asks herself about the happiness
of that sacred,
almost imaginary family.

II

She illuminates the good-byes of little Lila,
she remembers Claudito's kiss,
she remembers the feet, the water, the sound of the tender
river, and in her palms
the stones from the corners of each beloved pocket.
Then she turns on the night lights
and it seems as if she were undressing in a canvas of songs
and it seems as if they were crying.

III

Flying from their mouths
like birds
the names of the children
and of the children
of the others,
and the others
also repeat the names of the others
and of other children of others.
They look for each other.
They cry.
Abandoned, they gather together,
the Mothers of the Plaza de Mayo.

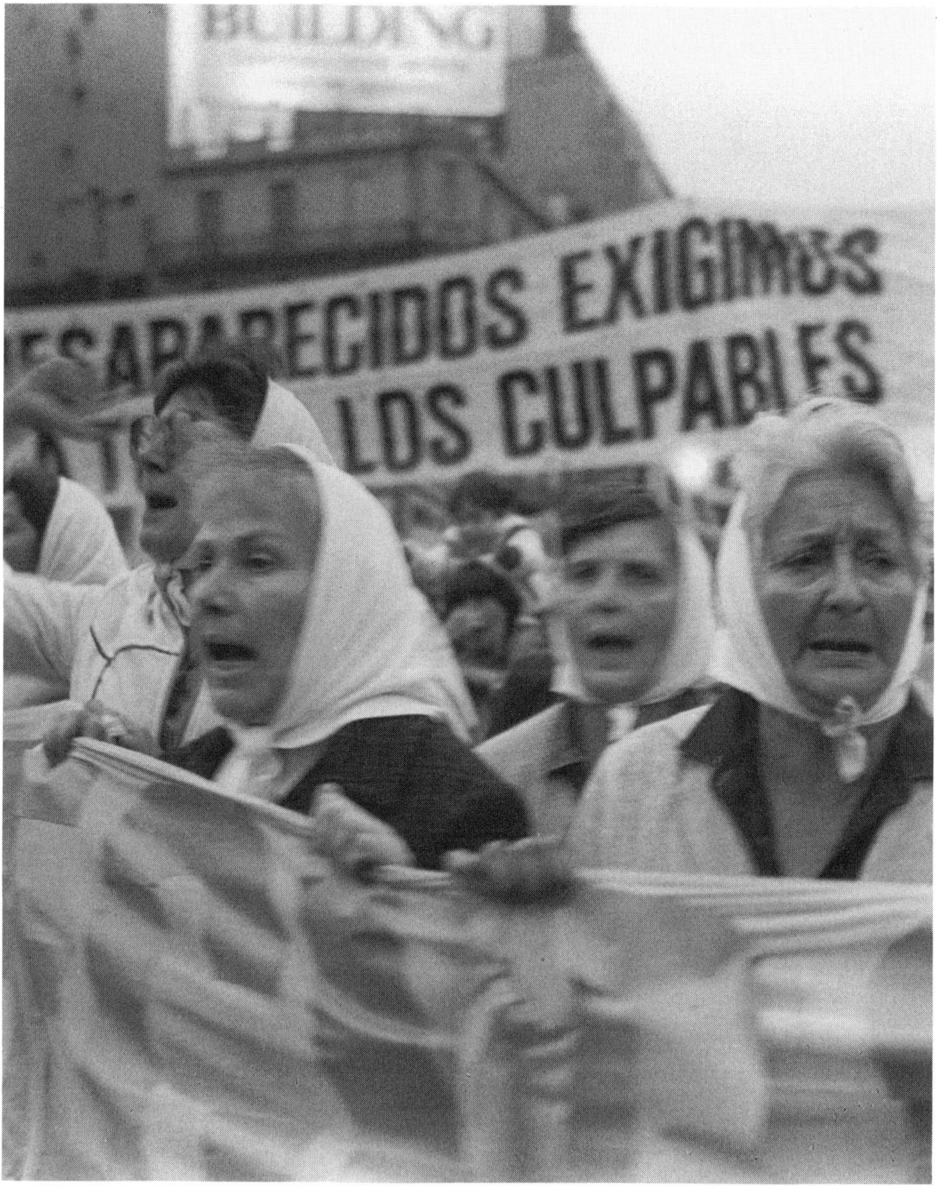
ESAPARECIDOS EXIGIMOS
LOS CULPABLES

MISTY LETTERS

Speechless and full of tenderness,
she reads the misty letters,
and the voices of the departed
flourish within her hardened skin.
It looks like she is playing tender tunes,
like she is listening to the words of the departed,
now distant, voiceless.
She reads and rereads, examines and lets go
the misty letters
and the laughter of the disappeared
watches over her, crowning her with birds.

CARTAS DE AGUA

Enmudecida repleta de ternura,
lee las cartas de agua,
y las voces de los idos
florecen en su piel de durezas.
Parece que está tocando ternuras,
que escucha las palabras de los idos, ya ajenos
enmudecida,
lee y relee, revisa, resalta
las cartas de agua,
y la risa de los desaparecidos
la vigila la puebla de pájaros.

KERCHIEFS

The kerchiefs that they tie, that are untied, madly whistle, kiss and moan. Give me a kerchief against injustice, give me a hand to stretch out so I may become a solitary lament that covers you. Give me a kerchief against injustice, so that I may be a white remnant of an absence, so that I will not be a foreigner of maimed bones. I want a kerchief against injustice so I can cover you, dance with you on the winged banners of peace, fill you up with caresses, and make you dream about a memory of your body very close to mine, as if we were two joining fountainheads.

PAÑUELOS

Los pañuelos que atan, que se desatan, enloquecidos silban, besan, gimen. Denme un pañuelo contra la injusticia, denme una mano para extenderme, para hacerme un solo quejido cubriéndote. Denme un pañuelo contra la injusticia, para ser el blanco retazo de una ausencia, para no ser una extranjera de huesos mancos. Yo quiero un pañuelo contra la injusticia, para cubrirte, para danzarte en los lienzos alados de la paz, para llenarte de caricias y hacerte soñar en una memoria de tu cuerpo así muy junto al mío, como si fuéramos los natalicios de los ríos.

¿Cuántas veces yo converso con mis muertos
y sus manos, son una textura hundida, y les pregunto cosas
y sus rostros son una memoria de llagas, y la noche
amenazándonos en su caída intempestuosa, pero yo converso con
mis muertos que a lo mejor son tuyos, y los cubro, los empapo
de mi sentir callado y de mis ojos parecidos a los alambres de la
sombra. Siempre me despido de ese cuerpo, de esos ojos que me parecen
un río de silencio.
Y así aprendo a decirles cosas,
a prometerles un jardín floreciente, florido,
una historia, un nacimiento, una promesa,
y es tan increíble como yo amo a este muerto, que no es mi
muerto,
que tampoco es un cadáver. Es un salto de agua, un diálogo,
una costa para cruzar.

How many times do I talk with my dead?
And their hands are rough and wrinkled, and I ask them
things and their faces are a memory of sorrows, and the night
threatens us in its tempestuous fall, but I talk with
my dead which perhaps are yours, and I cover them, saturate
them with my silent sorrow and with my tear-drenched eyes.
I always bid farewell to that body,
to those eyes that seem like a river
of silence.
And this is how I learn to tell them things,
to promise them a blossoming, flowery garden,
a history, a beginning, a promise,
and it is so incredible how I love this dead one, who is not mine,
who is not a cadaver either, but a waterfall, a dialog,
a shore to be crossed.

JUICIO
LOS
Quintana
María Tere
18 años
Alejandro Efrain
Ford
20 años
Obrero

They patiently name them, as if dealing with legends.
But they are their children and no one attends the ceremonies
and no one looks out of the antechambers of the departed.

Con paciencia ellas los nombran, como si se tratara de leyendas.
Pero son los hijos, y nadie asiste a las ceremonias y nadie se
asoma por las antesalas de los idos.

The jacarandás, spreading their scent, charming us with the tempestuous odor of their fragrance, distant like photographs of dislocated memories. The jacarandás, making alliances with the lovers or offering shade to the old passers-by. The jacarandás, covering coffins and omens, drawing me toward the portrait of my daughter Lila in an invisible city without a seashore. A concave and painful absence locked within my painful dreams.

Los jacarandás, esparciendo decires, hechizándonos con el olor intepestuoso de sus fragancias, lejanas como las fotografías de las memorias dislocadas. Los jacarandás, haciendo alianzas con los enamorados o sombra con los ancianos transeúntes. Los jacarandás, cubriendo ataúdes y presagios, acercándome al retrato de mi hija Lila, en una ciudad invisible sin mar. Cóncava ausencia dolida en los dolidos sueños.

DESFILES

Bajo sus ojos lleva las cicatrices de la ausencia y su caminar es
un juego de dados tambaleándose, fracturándose en los indicios
del miedo. Ella desfila, se alarga, y el dolor la extiende,
haciéndola cada vez más una inmensa pirámide de soles y
estiércoles. Dice que busca a sus vivos o a sus muertos. Y ella
desfila, se contornea, y su pañuelo es un solo delirio como las
señales de la muerte.
En la noche todo es ausencia y el día es una invención maldita.
No hay duelo para la buscadora.

Y el silencio de los cuerpos que anidan la acompaña
y la noche misma es un estrepitoso silencio dislocado, alado, es
cóncavo entre sus pasos de niebla.

PROCESSIONS

Beneath her eyes she carries the scars of absence, and her gait
is like a tottering game of dice rupturing in the vestiges
of fear. She marches, she stretches, and her grief expands,
increasingly transforming her into an immense pyramid of sunflowers
and dung. She says that she is looking for either her living or her dead.
And she marches and goes round, and her kerchief is a singular delirium,
like the signs of death.
At night all is absence, and the day is an evil invention.
There is no mourning for the seeker.

And the silence of the nested bodies accompanies her,
and night itself is a deafening, dislocated, winged silence,
a concave surface beneath her nebulous steps.

Vacíos para siempre han quedado
los armarios, y ella conversa en la orilla de una cama
que se escurre, flota, y es un oficio de tinieblas,
donde el cuerpo ido deja una huella que corroe
y ella, arqueada, palpa las camisas
y palpa las fotografías
de los nobles días de la vida.
Entonces se pone
a cantar
a pesar de las densas neblinas,
entonces se pone a cantar.

The closets have remained empty forever,
and she converses at the edge of a bed
that glides, floats, and is a ritual of darkness
where the absent body leaves an impression that corrodes,
and she, crouching, caresses the shirts,
and caresses the photographs
of the noble days of life.
And then she begins
to sing,
in spite of the dense mist,
then she begins to sing.

Y entonces las iluminadas hicieron altares. Una trajo un peine de nácar, otra un brillo de arena, una pala con estrellas. Entonces, una esperó hasta la médula misma de la oscuridad oscurísima, y comenzó a enterrar las prendas, los enormes suéteres tejidos a palillo, y la lana se tiñó de nácar, y el viento mismo la cubrió con la lana de estrellas. Entonces descansaron, dejaron de rondar enloquecidas, y alguien prendió unas velas para acompañar a los vivos.

And then the visionaries made altars. One brought a mother-of-pearl comb, another a shining grain of sand, a shovel full of stars. Then one waited until the very heart of darkness and began to bury the tokens and the enormous hand-knitted sweaters, their wool stained like mother-of-pearl, and the wind covered her with its blanket of stars. Then they rested, they stopped hovering like madwomen, and someone lighted candles to accompany the living.

Y entonces se lanzaban en el aire denso, alguien las
quemaba, sajándolas, rapándolas,
y parecían unas personas de plumas, jamás altivas, arrastrándose
para que la muerte alada no se las llevase, y danzaban con un
rito parecido a los delirios.
Entonces llevaban pañuelos blancos, de la misma forma en que
se lleva un amor.

And then they were hurled into the dense air, someone was
burning them, cutting them, shaving them,
and they seemed like feathered beings, never lofty,
crawling, so that winged death would not carry them off
and they danced in a ceremonial delirium.

Then they wore white kerchiefs, the same way
love is worn.

La vieron sujetar a su mismísima cintura y el roce de sus manos alargaba sus formas dislocadas. Parecía un espejo de agua, solísima, contemplando, y no sabían si hacer los bailes del duelo o de la vida. Y ella no sabía si era una danzante de agua o una estremecida madre sujetándose el desgarro de esos nacimientos, o al hijo que mecía muerto en sus sueños—memoria—en su país de humo.

They saw her grasp her own waist, and the friction from her hands length-
ened her dislocated form. She seemed like a looking-glass of water, contem-
plating, all alone, and they didn't know whether to have a dance of grief
or of life. And she didn't know whether she was a water dancer or a trem-
bling mother, holding on to the laceration of those births or to the son she
rocked dead in her dreams—a memory—in her land of smoke.

La niebla iracunda precisa asomándose por las hendiduras del jardín, a lo lejos alguien canta una memoria de lilas, alguien se pregunta por los pétalos del ensueño. Alguien dice, con una voz de mujer extraviada, que la loca plantaba lilas en el medio del musgo habitado, y entre los jardines, se asoman los niños muertos porque no quieren estar muertos, porque aún quieren vestirse y ser lilas, y las locas ellas, ellas las locas, matutinas, como si fueran espejos de clarividencias-claroscuras, se asoman, y los acechan tras los rosales, debajo de las amapolas, porque ¿quién no tiene un niño detrás de un manojo de esperanzas? ¿Quién no ha visto a un niño detrás de la anchura de los árboles?

The irascible distinct mist peeks through the crevices of the garden. In the distance someone sings a memory of lilies, and someone else asks for the petals of a daydream. Someone with a deranged woman's voice says the madwoman would plant lilies in the middle of spreading moss, and that the dead children appear in the gardens because they don't want to be dead, because they still want to dress up and be lilies, and the madwomen, the matutinal madwomen, appear like mirrors of clairvoyant chiaroscuros, and they watch them from behind the rose bushes and from beneath the poppies because who doesn't have a child behind a handful of hope? Who has not seen a child hiding behind a tree trunk?

COMO LA SUAVIDAD DE LOS COMIENZOS

I
Entonces el despertar del alba intrépida
y ahí están, somos
fotografías inmóviles
sobre unas llagas movedizas.
Ahí están las fotos estáticas, acechándola,
mirándola mientras obstinada sacude los muebles y entran por los
umbrales los vientos de los desaparecidos.

II
Se dirige a los armarios,
a las camas,
asea
una casa que gime
donde nadie llega ni regresa, ni golpea
tan sólo los vientos de los desaparecidos.

III
Ella igual busca,
apaga la luz, el hueso de la memoria
no duerme,
los saluda,
sólo fotos, estampas anonadadas.
Y los vientos de los desaparecidos
la golpean.

AS GENTLE AS BEGINNINGS

I
The intrepid dawn awakens
and here they are, we are
motionless photographs
on shifting sorrows.
Here are the still photos, watching her,
looking at her as she obstinately dusts the furniture
and the spirits of the disappeared come through the door.

II
She goes to the closets,
to the beds,
she cleans
a house that moans,
where no one arrives, returns, or knocks,
except for the spirits of the disappeared.

III
She also searches,
turns off the light, and in the depths of memory
does not sleep.
She greets them,
only photos, annihilated prints,
and the spirits of the disappeared
wound her.

Y estaban,
en los nichos o en las criptas de lo más mudo,
cada una de ellas insistía en precisar miradas,
un hombre, sujetando otra mano, ella con pan en los brazos,
dibujaban el cielo con la memoria,
y armaban los rostros con los pedazos perdidos
como quien se pone a tejer las cavidades, las
quebraduras, un eclipse de vidrios cortados, requebrados una
y otra vez,
y ellas tranquilas, como caracoles, arrastrándose, recostándose,
perdiéndose en el deseo
querían
que aparecieran
con vida, con luz, con vida viva
¿cómo hacer de aquellos trozos de manos solitarias insondables,
un ser, una iluminación de palabras,
una infancia germinando en las trincheras?
Entonces, ellas sólo dibujan a un cuerpo sobre el pavimento,
y lo desnudan en los nudos de tiza, blanca,
y del pavimento mismo nacen ruidos, quejidos que nadie sabe,
que nadie quiere, que nadie pregunta.
¿Y, cómo hablar de los muertos?

And they were
in the recesses or the crypts of the most silent,
each one of them insisting on specifying images,
a man, holding another hand, a woman with bread in her arms,
they drew the sky with their memories
and formed faces out of missing pieces
like someone who begins weaving holes,
fractures, an eclipse of cut glass broken over
and over again,
and peaceful as snails, creeping, reclining and
losing themselves in desire,
they wanted
them to appear
with life, with light, with vivid life.
How can
a being, an illumination of words,
a childhood sprouting in the ditches
be made from those fragments of solitary, unreachable hands?
So they only draw the outline of a body on the pavement,
they lay it bare in lumps of white chalk,
and from the pavement arise noises and laments that
no one knows, that no one wants, that no one questions.
For how do you talk about the dead?

Una mujer aguarda a sus muertos, en un comedor
insensato. Aulla esos nombres como los dados de la muerte; se
resfriega los ojos y pide verlos mejor,
decirles cosas como el color del cielo en los parques,
o el porqué de las lluvias en una mirada.
Una mujer habla de la muerte como si fuera una vagabunda en
rotaciones ancladas.
Una mujer conversa con la muerte en
un comedor de sillas mancas, de
tenedores carmesíes, un cuchillo
solitario
desfila en la penumbra
Una mujer aguarda a sus muertos.

A woman waits for her dead in a useless
dining room. She howls those names
like the dice of death; she clears her eyes
and asks to see them better,
to tell them things like the color of the sky
in the parks,
or the reason for her tear-drenched look.
A woman talks about death as if it were a vagabond
moving in a tethered circle.
A woman converses with death in
a dining room of maimed chairs,
scarlet colored forks, and a
solitary knife
marching in the semi-darkness.
A woman waits for her dead.

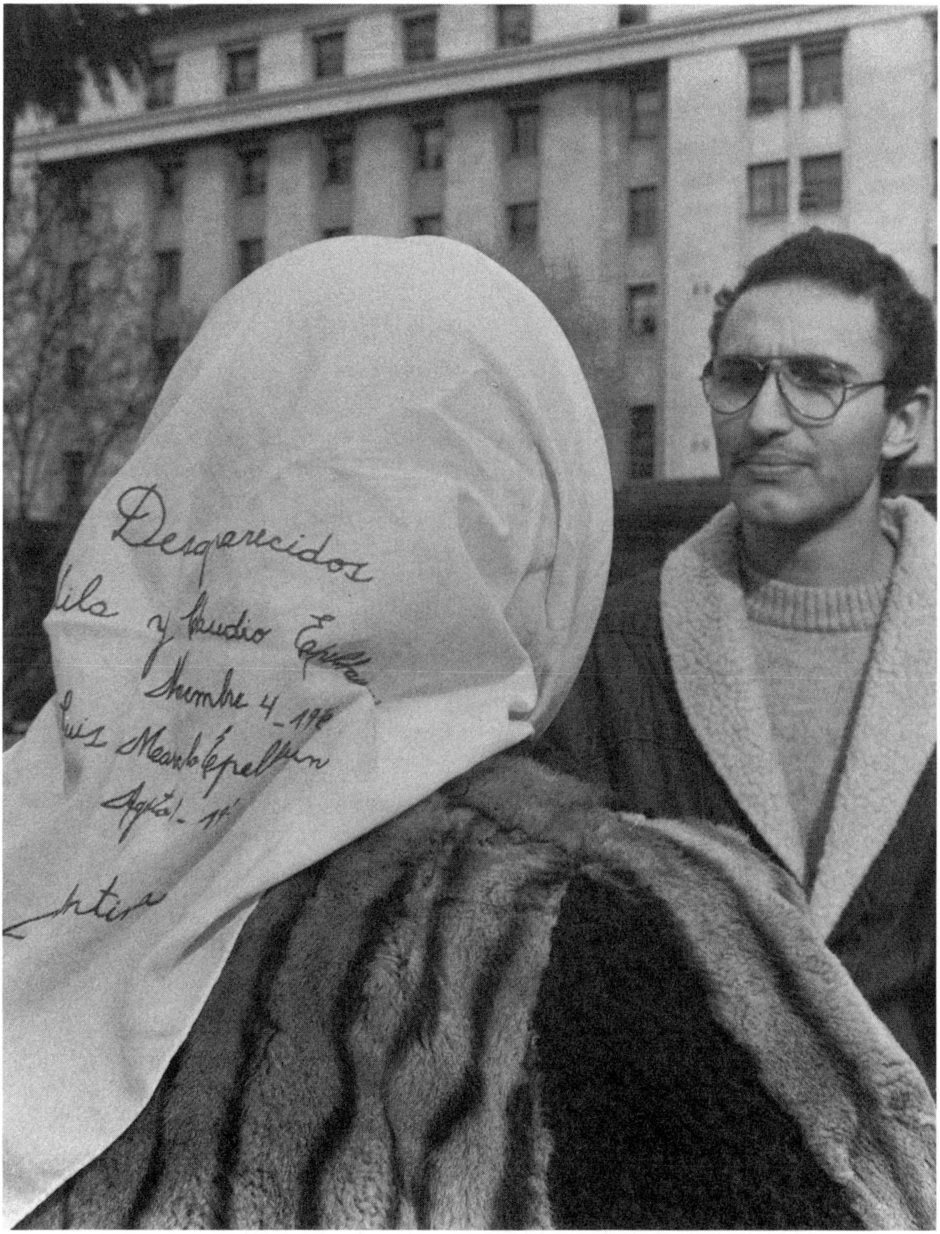
Desaparecidos

De puntillas se alzaban, ebrias en su fatalidad, y cada pisada dejaba las huellas de un insomnio. Extrañamente, sus pañuelos parecían ser alas o el sonido de la lluvia, transmutado en neblinas, y así iban las brujas de la verdad, deslizándose, inventando clarividencias ingenuas. Parecían ser una sola banda de aves, victimarias y magas. Ahí estaban detenidas, movedizas, extrañas forasteras. Y la plaza era una fiesta iluminada.

They arose on tiptoe, intoxicated in their doom, and each footstep left behind traces of insomnia. Strangely, their kerchiefs seemed like wings or like the sound of falling rain transmuted into mist, and this is how the witches of truth went about, slipping away and inventing ingenuous visions. They seemed like a solitary flock of birds, assassins, and wizards. There they were, timid, unsteady, and strange outsiders. And the plaza was a feast of lights.

Comienzan a moverse, lentas, lentísimas. Alguien las suspende desde la altura misma de los pies. Parecen danzar y trenzarse hacia la deriva. Míralas cómo se estremecen para construir rondas y bailan cada vez más afiebradas, poseídas, en la raíz misma de una locura enfermiza. Bailan alrededor de los muertos, exigen espacios, piden saber, y bailan, y bailan como si fuera este baile el último round del alma.

They begin to move slowly, sluggishly, as if someone were suspending them from high above. They seem to dance and to swagger off course. Look at them and how they quiver to form circles and each time they dance more feverishy, possessed, near the very root of a sickly madness. They dance around the dead, they demand space, they demand to know, and they dance, and they dance as if this dance were the last round of their souls.

I

Hermana amada,
mujer de cicatrizes y solsticios
amiga de los pordioseros
eterna compañera de los torturados
'ven, ayúdame en la amanecida.
Déjame poner un sueño en tus faldas
que lavaron el dolor agrio, inundado, de los despellejados.

II

Déjame morirme
en tus brazos de sol y sangre que se
deshacen para volver a llenarse
de veranos fresas, y pieles alegres del Sur.

III

Amiga mía,
hermana,
amada danzarina de las fuentes,
de los cuerpos que acechan la extensión del amor,
déjame ser palabra en tu ausencia.

IV

Amada, mientras alzas tus manos
y tus palmas son los senderos,
los ríos, las historias de luces y luciérnagas
madre amada
compañera de planetas, duelos y nacimientos
verde, verdosa dama
déjame ser
tu hija.

I

Beloved sister,
woman of scars and solstices
friend of beggars
eternal companion of the tortured
come, help me at the break of dawn.
In your skirts that washed the bitter,
inundated grief of the despoiled,
let me place a dream.

II

Let me die
in your arms of sunlight and blood that
dissolve to fill up again
with summer strawberries and bright southern hides.

III

My friend,
sister
beloved dancer of the fountains
and of the bodies that wait for love's embrace,
let me be the word in your absence.

IV

Beloved, as you raise your hands
and your palms become the trails,
the rivers, the stories of light and fireflies,
beloved mother,
companion of planets, tribulations and births,
green, greenish lady
let me be
your daughter.

Maga vidente
violada cada tres segundos
déjame ponerte una colcha de sueños,
déjame hacer con el cuerpo
una playa, un girasol, los vientos de la delicia
porque en tus manos anidan
los sin puertas,
los que ocupan el espacio
de las aceras agrietadas,
porque en tu palabra,
aparecen los muertos-vivos
jamás igualados,
jamás enterrados,
los muertos,
que ocupan tus llagas en las miradas,
los muertos, que cabalgan en tus alientos,
y te besan tus pechos con tanta sed y sangre.
Madre amada,
eres un faro con ritmo de gaviota
una ruta secreta con tus anhelos bordados
con nombres de vivos y muertos,
muertos y vivos,
déjame llorar en tus tinieblas,
bañarme en la luz de la victoria silenciosa.

Luminous sage
desecrated every three seconds
let me cover you with a blanket of dreams,
let me make your body
a seashore, a sunflower, winds of delight
because in your hands live
the homeless,
those that occupy the space
of the cracked sidewalks,
because in your word
appear the living dead,
never equaled,
never buried,
the dead,
that live in your looks of pain,
the dead,
that ride in your breaths
and kiss your breasts with so much thirst and blood.
Beloved mother,
you are a beacon with a seagull's rhythm,
a secret route with your desires embroidered with
the names of the living and the dead,
the dead and the living,
let me cry in your darknes,
and bathe in the light of silent victory.

MEMORIAL

La memoria como un trozo de lienzo impreciso y bello
acumulando los rescoldos de la ira,
las bellezas de una ternura amplia y
dibujada
en la raíz misma de una espada de fe se extiende para
ser una mesa donde
cada uno escribe lo que quiere
o no quiere recordar:
una espalda de madera lisa para inventar los
mapas de las cosas queridas,
la memoria volando en el revés mismo del cielo
oscura y luminosa
doblada y siempre
haciéndose a sí misma
como un collar de palabras
entre las piedras cautivadas,
las que nada pueden decir.

MEMORIAL

Memory, like a piece of beautiful and imprecise canvas
accumulating the embers of wrath,
the beauties of an expansive tenderness that is
stretched
to the very base of a sword of faith which expands
to become a table where
everyone writes what he wants
or does not want to remember:
a blade of smooth wood where we can invent
maps of our most cherished possessions,
memory flying opposite the sky,
dark and luminous,
folded and always
transforming itself
into a necklace of words
strung between the captive stones
that cannot say anything.

Las flores amarillas
destapadas resposando sobre las yerbas sedosas
parecen ser las faldas que el viento levanta y trepa
y soplan en una luz tenue de gracias secretas
y adivinan los sueños de los desvalidos
espectadores
de las mujeres solísimas
que buscan una flor amarilla de la amanecida
en sus contornos
que buscan una ráfaga de amarillos
para las tumbas
sin nombre.

The yellow flowers
uncovered and resting on the silken grass
seem like skirts that the wind lifts and mounts
and they blow in a tenuous light of secret graces,
foretelling the dreams of the unprotected
spectators,
of the very lonely women
who watch from their outposts
for a yellow flower of dawn,
who look for a gust of yellow blossoms
for the tombs
of the nameless.

Ella es un soliloquio entre sus pasos, una alquimia de la vida misma, erguida, descalza, altísima en su silencio y en la plenitud de sus inmensas abiertas palmas. Va hacia el río, un abrazo de agua marca sus travesías y en el río ondulado leve, ella alza sus manos, para encontrarlo, hallarlo, decirle en el oído los sonidos del agua y ella se transforma en árbol, porque sus brazos son dos ramas floridas mientras lo busca en el río, y cuando no aparece entonces, ella se acerca al mar, a los inmensos territorios de las costas y al aliento indomable de la deriva.

A veces ya no divisa al río o lo confunde con la plena mar. A veces, regresa descalza en una sola caricia mojada y sueña con las penas, y sueña con ir otra vez veloz al río porque a lo mejor verá sus cabellos castaños, soleados, si no está en el río, a lo mejor, sí, seguro que estará en el mar. Si no estará en el mar, seguro en el cielo de la tierra.

Walking, she is a soliloquy, an alchemy of life itself, erect, barefoot, majestic in her silence and in the plenitude of her immense open palms. She goes to the river; an embrace of water outlines her crossings, and in the light rippling river, she raises her hands to find him, to discover him, and to whisper water sounds in his ear, and she becomes a tree because her arms are two flowery branches while she looks for him, and when he does not appear, she then approaches the sea, the immense territories of the coasts and the dauntless vigor of the surging tide.

Sometimes she no longer sees the river or she confuses it with the whole sea. Sometimes she returns barefoot in a lonely wet caress and dreams about her sorrows, and she dreams about returning quickly to the river because maybe she will see his brown sun-bleached locks of hair, and if he is not in the river, maybe, yes, surely he will be in the sea. If he isn't in the sea, surely he will be in heaven.

APARICION CON VIDA
CASTIGO A LOS CULPABLES
MADRES DE PLAZA DE MAYO
EL PAIS FRENTE A LA HIPOCRESIA OFICIAL Y LA SOBERBIA MILITAR
PUNTO FINAL
PIRME UN PAÑUELO CONTRA LA INJUSTICIA
MADRES DE PLAZA DE MAYO
ADRES DE
ZA. DE MAYO

SONIDOS

Las palabras se desgarraron del sonido.
Emigraron feroces en el comienzo de mi labio.
Cosas extrañas se colaban en mi sed,
flores no fecundadas
hervían en mi paladar
amordazado.
Emigré de mí misma,
quise condenarme en el abecedario de las mudas,
para así no gritar
así no aullar
para así decir sin el decir.
Las palabras desgarraron la oscuridad de mi tiniebla enmudecida.
Quise ser entonces
la palabra misma de la voz
repetir un nombre.

SOUNDS

The words broke away from the sound.
They emigrated ferociously to the edge of my lips.
Strange things filtered into my thirst, fruitless
flowers seethed in my
silenced palate.
I emigrated from myself;
I tried to condemn myself to the language of the deaf,
so as not to cry out,
so as not to wail,
so as to tell without telling.
The words tore into the obscurity of my silenced darkness.
Then I tried to be
the spoken word,
so I could repeat a name.

POEMA PARA RECITAR IN LOS SUEÑOS DEL MAR

Y en la noche, los sonidos de la noche ocre y alucinada, destartalada e imprecisa; y en la noche ella busca una memoria, y se llama en voz alta y se acaricia el pelo hasta hacerse una herida, siempre en las manos. Y los sonidos de la noche, la acercan a otras noches y a noches parecidas a las maderas húmedas, parecidas a las casas que aguardan a sus huéspedes para colmarlos de una luz como las estaciones invencibles del sueño.

POEM TO BE RECITED IN DREAMS OF THE SEA

At night, in the sounds of an ocher and hallucinatory, confused and imprecise night, she searches for a memory and shouts her name and caresses her hair until a wound appears, always in her hands. And the night sounds draw her closer to other nights, to nights resembling humid wood piles, resembling homes that wait for their guests to adorn them with light like the invincible seasons of dream.

Las madres de los presos políticos
no se endurecen ni llevan en sus
rostros las huellas y trazos del dolor
las mujeres de los presos
políticos llevan el pan de la victoria
cuando se acercan por las rendijas aterradoras del vacío
y cuando reparten pan, maíz, y sol,
la cárcel se llena de pájaros y brazos cantores
las mujeres de los presos políticos
no lloran cuando se despiden
de los maridos condenados a muerte
de los recientemente torturados
ellas cantan un himno parecido
a los diluvios o a los profundos arcoiris
de las delicias
y se van
marchando
y entre sus faldas
germinan niños
y en vez de incendios y lápidas
se repiten como los ríos y la vida
y no son nada de parecidas
a los tacones solapados de
la muerte.

Mothers of political prisoners
do not get hardhearted, nor do they carry in their
faces traces and outlines of pain.
Women of political prioners
carry victory bread
when they approach the terrifying cracks of the void
and when they hand out bread, corn, and sunshine,
the prison fills up with birds and singing arms.
Women of political prisoners
don't cry when they bid farewell
to their spouses condemned to death,
to the recently tortured.
They sing a hymn that resembles
floods or deep rainbows
of delight
and they leave
marching
and between their skirts
sprout children
and instead of fires and gravestones
they repeat themselves like rivers and life
and they don't seem anything
like the furtive heels of
death.

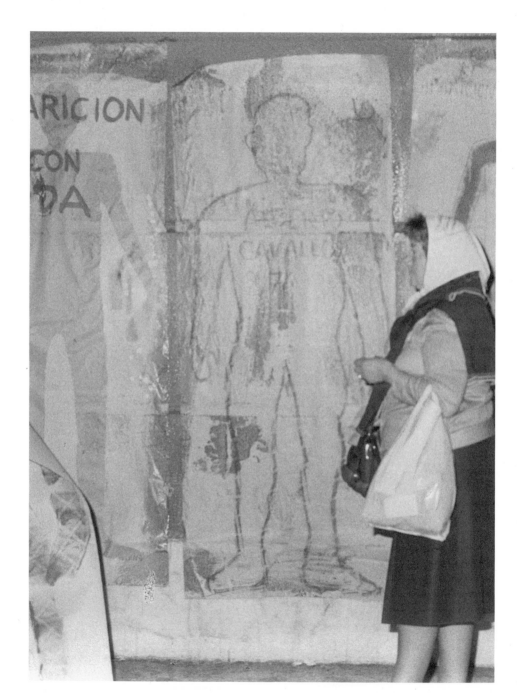

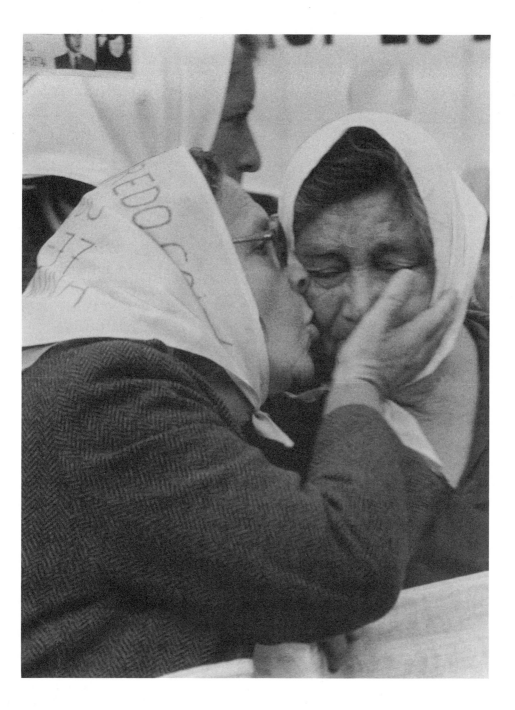

Transparentes,
los cofres de la memoria.
El aire se vuelve hundido
en su frente que arde y clama.
Su vista hinchada es una sola mirada de espanto,
un huracán de ojos detenidos.
Ella saca las cartas
de sus tres muertos
o vivos,
y una voz de música y esencia
y un amanecer de agua los envuelve.
Todo se ancla en el silencio
y ella camina tranquila
errando los cofres,
cerrando el incendio
de sus ojos que palpitan presencias.

Transparent
coffers of memory.
The air becomes deep-set
in her burning and clamoring forehead.
Her swollen glance is a solitary look of fright,
a hurricane of shiftless eyes.
She gets the letters
of her three dead
or live ones,
and a voice of music and fragrance
and a dawn of water surrounds them.
Everything is anchored in silence
and she walks peacefully
missing the coffers,
and putting out the fire
in her eyes that throb with presences.

Y sus labios comenzaban a abrirse muy lentamente como si fueran magas salidas
de un sueño herido y había en ellas el movimiento de pájaras incendiadas.
Caminaban confundiéndose con los gestos de los árboles que parecían hijos
meciéndose y era una sola muchedumbre transparente mientras espectadores
    y
difuntos huían aterrados. Las sabias magas que parecían sombras aclaradas por
la misma luz que las sujetaba, comenzaron a pedir cosas: una decía "háblame,
háblame," y otra llamaba a un niño perdido.
Todos sus cuerpos se doblaban
y no por el viento
ni por los árboles que las envolvía cada vez más estrechamente cuando
llamaban. Eran mujeres jóvenes con niños en los brazos.
Yo tampoco las pude dejar de pensar
porque parecían huérfanas que me llamaban
y decían
no me dejes
yo no podía no ser algo de ellas, ni dejarlas,
porque sería como dejar
a mi madre
sin sus huesos,
sin hija
dejarlas así, todas abiertas y llenas
de valles oscuros.
Entonces yo también comencé a acercarme,
a pronunciar algo que me mordía desde muy adentro.
Y mientras oía, oíamos el ulular de las sirenas
y mis labios también se convirtieron en pájaros
y mis manos en árboles
y mis palabras
en miles de rostros.

And their lips began to open very slowly as if they were
sages escaping from a wounded dream, and in them was
a movement of burning birds. They walked confusing
themselves with the gestures of the trees that seemed like
children rocking, and it was a single transparent crowd
while spectators and corpses fled in terror. The wise
sages seemed like shadows clarified by the
same light that subdued them, and they began to ask for
things. One said "talk to me, talk to me,"
the other called out to a lost child.
All their bodies bent
not because of the wind
nor because of the trees that surrounded them more
each time they called. They were
young women with children in their arms.
I also could not stop thinking of them
because they seemed like orphans calling me
and saying
don't leave me.
I could not refrain from becoming part of them, nor
could I abandon them,
because it would be like leaving
my own mother
without her bones,
without her daughter,
leaving them like this, everyone open and full
of obscure valleys.
Then I also began to approach,
to give voice to something that was eating me away inside.
And while I listened we heard the screeching of sirens
and my lips became birds
and my hands, trees
and my words
thousands of faces.

A NEW PRAISE OF FOLLY

The first was written many years ago by Erasmus of Rotterdam. I don't remember well what it was about, but its title always moved me, and now I know why: folly deserves to be praised when reason, that reason which fills the West with so much pride, breaks its teeth against a reality which does not allow itself, nor will it ever allow itself, to be trapped by the cold arms of logic, pure science, and technology.

From Jean Cocteau is this profound intuition that many prefer to ascribe to his supposed frivolity: Victor Hugo was a madman who believed himself to be Victor Hugo. Nothing more true: one must be brilliant—an epithet that to me always seemed to be a reasonable euphemism to explain the ultimate degree of madness, that is, the breakdown of all reasonable connections—in order to write *Toilers of the Sea* and *Notre Dame of Paris.* On the day in which the penpushers and hired assassins of the Argentine military junta began circulating the term "madwomen'to neutralize and ridicule the Mothers of the Plaza de Mayo, it would have been more to their benefit to think about what follows, supposing that they had been capable of such thoughts, which, itself, is quite improbable. Fools, as corresponds to their stock and inclinations, they didn't realize that they were hurling into flight an enormous flock of doves that would cover the earth's heavens with its message of anguished truth, with a message that each day is heard more and understood more by the free peoples of the world.

Since I am not at all a politician and very much a poet, I perceive historical discourse like the Japanese calligraphers perceived their drawings: there is a sheet of paper that represents both space and time, and there is a stylus that a hand briefly lets run across the page in order to draw signs that link together, that play with one another, that look for their own harmony and that interrupt themselves at the exact point which they, themselves, determine. I am very well aware that there is a dialectics of history (I would not be a socialist if I did not believe it), but I also know that this dialectics of human societies is not the cold logical product that so many theoreticians of history and politics would like it to be. The irrational, the unexpected, the flock of doves, the Mothers of the Plaza de Mayo, burst forth at any moment to thwart and disturb the most scientific calculations of our schools of war and national security. This is why I am not afraid to add myself to the list of madmen when I say in a way that will make many of the well-thinking grind their teeth, that the succession of General Viola by General Galtieri is today the obvious product and significant triumph of that throng of mothers and grandmothers who have persisted for such a long time in visiting the Plaza de Mayo for reasons that don't have anything to do with aedilian charms or the more ashen majesty of its celebrated obelisk.

In the past few months a more defined outlook of a significant segment of the Argentine nation has either consciously or unconsciously supported the mad obstinacy of a handful of women who demand explanations for the dissapearances of their loved ones. Shame, a force that can hide itself for a long time, explodes in the end in the most unexpected ways, and this is something that has never been taken into account by the wisdom of the military men in power. That under the less violent rule of Viola that outburst has assumed the magnitude of a demonstration of thousands upon thousands of Argentines in the central avenues of Buenos Aires, and in a rising series of declarations, denouncements and petitions in the newspapers, is proof of the military weakness that the line of Galtieri and other warhawks could not tolerate. They, of course, don't understand it very clearly, but the logic of madness isn't less implacable than that which is studied in military school: the corollary of the theorem is that General Galtieri should be recognized by the Mothers of the Plaza de Mayo, for it is above all thanks to them that he has been able to inflict the blow that has finally raised him to the position of commander-in-chief.

The mothers and the grandmothers, for their part and without knowing it, have expedited his rise to power, without having the least idea that they have done this. Far to the contrary, for on the plane of immediate reality, that substitution of command signifies a profound aggravation of the sociopolitical panorama of Argentina. However, that aggravation is simultaneously the proof that the glass is even fuller, and that the process is reaching its point of maximum tension. It is then that the response of that part of our nation still capable of feeling shame should enter into action through all possible avenues, and that the internal and external forces of the country will have to respond to something that is inviting them to depart from an era that is quite explainable—but that cannot continue without giving reason to those who pretend to possess it.

Let's continue in our folly, mothers and dear grandmothers of the Plaza de Mayo, people of the pen and of the word, exiles from within and from without. Argentines, let's continue in our folly: there is no other way to put an end to that reason that vociferates its slogans of order, discipline, and patriotism. Let's continue hurling the doves of the true country into the skies of our motherland and into those of the whole world.

—Julio Cortázar
1984